VITAL TO EARTH!
Keystone Species Explained

T0024732

BEES

IN THEIR ECOSYSTEMS

by Olivia Hammond

BEARPORT
PUBLISHING

Minneapolis, Minnesota

Credits
Cover and title page, © Geoff Smith/Alamy; 4–5, © Serhii Ivankin/iStock; 7, © fpwing/Getty; 9, © Uwe Nake/iStock; 10–11, © PictureBookz/iStock; 12–13, © tracielouise/iStock; 14, © Kuttelvaserova Stuchelova/Shutterstock; 14–15, © stock_colors/iStock; 16, © duncan1890/iStock; 17, © Sabena Jane Blackbird/Alamy; 18, © kosobu/iStock; 18–19, © Picture Partners/AdobeStock; 20–21, © zhongguo/ iStock; 22–23, © Chris Robbins/Alamy; 24–25, © Ramdan_Nain/iStock; 26–27, © Olga Kaya/iStock; 28, © egon69/iStock; 29T, © raferto/iStock; 29TM, © peplow/iStock; 29M, © proxyminder/iStock; 29BM, © AscentXmedia/iStock; 29B, © monkeybusinessimages/iStock.

Bearport Publishing Company Product Development Team
President: Jen Jenson; Director of Product Development: Spencer Brinker; Managing Editor: Allison Juda; Associate Editor: Naomi Reich; Associate Editor: Tiana Tran; Art Director: Colin O'Dea; Designer: Elena Klinkner; Designer: Kayla Eggert; Product Development Assistant: Owen Hamlin

STATEMENT ON USAGE OF GENERATIVE ARTIFICIAL INTELLIGENCE
Bearport Publishing remains committed to publishing high-quality nonfiction books. Therefore, we restrict the use of generative AI to ensure accuracy of all text and visual components pertaining to a book's subject. See BearportPublishing.com for details.

Library of Congress Cataloging-in-Publication Data is available at www.loc.gov or upon request from the publisher.

ISBN: 979-8-88916-632-0 (hardcover)
ISBN: 979-8-88916-639-9 (paperback)
ISBN: 979-8-88916-645-0 (ebook)

For more information, write to Bearport Publishing, 5357 Penn Avenue South, Minneapolis, MN 55419.

Contents

World-Building Bees

In springtime, bright green plants and blossoming flowers coat the world in color. Animals move through this new growth, looking for food. Hummingbirds fuel up on sweet **nectar**. Hungry bears roam in search of berries and honey. A hawk swoops down to catch a mouse that has left its leafy shelter to snack on seeds.

Through it all, tiny buzzing creatures flit from flower to flower. Though they are small, bees are mighty. They are a big reason this meadow is brimming with life. Bees are vital to their **ecosystems**.

There are more than 20,000 **species** of bees around the world. They can be found on every continent except Antarctica. The buzzing insects live in many kinds of habitats, including forests, meadows, prairies, and wetlands.

A Key Animal

Busy, buzzing bees are a keystone species—a kind of plant or animal that is crucial to supporting an entire community within an area. These species shape the land or help balance the populations of plants and animals in a way that benefits everything in the ecosystem.

When bees are removed from their habitats, plants can't grow and develop. Soon, other creatures no longer have their food or shelter. Without bees, life on Earth would struggle to survive.

Most kinds of bees live alone. They come together only to have young. Social bees, on the other hand, live and work in groups known as **colonies**. They raise young together.

Bumblebees and honeybees are two kinds of social bees.

Bees Need Flowers

Bees and flowering plants have a long history together. In fact, the buzzing insects first appeared about 125 million years ago alongside Earth's first blossoms. Bees feed from flowers.

The animals buzz from plant to plant, looking for nectar—the sweet drink found in flowers—to sip. This gives the insects their energy. The flying creatures also collect the plants' **pollen**, which provides bees with protein to stay strong and healthy. Both forms of food help bees survive and raise their young.

Honeybees turn the natural sugars from nectar into honey through a process that involves partially digesting the nectar and mixing it with an **enzyme** from the bees' bodies.

Pollen sticks to little hairs
on a bee as it moves
around the flower.

Flowers Need Bees

Bees don't just take from flowers. The insects and plants are **mutualists**. This means they each give something in the relationship. Bees help flowering plants, and the plants provide food for the insects.

Bees are some of the planet's best pollinators. To get all the food they need, bees must visit many flowers—sometimes thousands in a day! As they go from flower to flower, some of the pollen they collect from one rubs off onto the next. This pollinates the flowers, allowing them to create new life. The flowers develop into seeds, nuts, fruits, and vegetables. These can then go on to create more plants.

Other insects, birds, and bats also move pollen from one flower to the next. However, bees are responsible for pollinating up to 80 percent of the world's flowering plants.

Feeding the Food Web

By helping plants grow, bees provide the framework for complex food webs that connect all living things. The plants bees pollinate make the food that many animals—from bugs to birds and rabbits to squirrels—need to survive. Other animals go on to eat the plant eaters, eventually supporting all life in the ecosystem.

Bees themselves are also a direct source of food for some creatures. Skunks, beetles, and many birds snack on these insects as a part of their diet.

Every food web needs producers. These are living things that can make, or produce, their own food. Plants are the producers in most food webs. Bees help these producers **reproduce**.

Many birds eat berries that grow
after bees pollinate flowers.

Making a Home

Plant growth that happens thanks to pollination also creates a place for many creatures to live and raise their young. As plants are pollinated, they spread. Some of the seeds of fruits, vegetables, and nuts end up back in the ground for new plants to grow from.

These healthy, robust plants provide many animals with shelters. Thick growth keeps the worst of the weather away. It helps hide many **prey** creatures from hungry **predators**. Here, animals can safely protect eggs and raise their young out of view.

Honeybees build hives where they live, work, raise young, and store honey. Sometimes, mice, moths, and ants use empty or poorly defended hives as a shelter or a safe space to lay eggs.

Hedgehogs benefit from the plants bees pollinate.

Bringing the Bees to America

Humans have long known the value of bees. Within about a decade of first arriving in the Americas, European settlers began bringing honeybees across the ocean to help them build a new life. Unlike **native** bees, which pollinate wild plants, these honeybees were **domesticated**. They were kept and managed by people. Settlers raised and kept colonies, or groups of bees, in wooden hives near their fruit and vegetable crops. They gathered honey from these hives.

Honeybees were shipped from England to what would become Virginia in early 1622, with more following soon after. This started the long history of domesticated bees in the Americas.

Inside their hives, bees store honey in honeycombs.

Helping Humans

Farmers today still bring these busy, buzzing pollinators to their farms. One-third of the food we eat comes from crops pollinated by honeybees. Domesticated bees help farmers grow almonds, apples, melons, pumpkins, blueberries, and cherries. They even pollinate the clover and alfalfa that feed many of our farm animals.

And the benefits of honeybees don't stop there. Honey and beeswax can be used to make sugar, candles, and a polish for furniture and leather. Bee **venom** can even be used in medicines!

There are millions of honeybee colonies in North America. Each colony can contain tens of thousands of bees. That adds up to more than 100 billion honeybees on the continent!

Losing Their Home

Despite how important they are, bees are in trouble. Today, as much as 40 percent of bee species face the risk of **extinction**. Many of the wild, open spaces where native bees once ate their fill have been taken over by humans. Flowering landscapes have been transformed into cities or farmlands. This loss of land is shrinking bees' food supply, giving them fewer options and making their diets less **nutritious**.

The plants that do remain are not always safe for bees. The insects are being poisoned by **pesticides** and other chemicals used on farm crops and lawns. Many kinds of native bees are disappearing.

Some native bees pollinate only one kind of plant. If those plants disappear, so do the bees. If the bees disappear, the plants cannot reproduce.

About 99 percent of the grasslands across the American Midwest have been lost to farms, houses, and businesses.

Sick and Tired

Even though they are cared for by humans, honeybees are also in trouble. Like native bees, they are at risk due to an increasingly restricted diet. They are also being poisoned by pesticides that farmers and homeowners use on their crops, gardens, and yards.

In addition, parasites, pests, and pathogens have led to the failure of many honeybee colonies. Small mites enter honeybee hives, feeding on the bees and spreading diseases as they invade. Bacteria and fungi can easily kill whole colonies.

Domesticated honeybees brought to a farm to pollinate crops can spread diseases to wild bees in the area. They can also infect wasps, ants, and some kinds of flies.

Mite

Varroa mites feed on bees. They often carry viruses that might kill the entire colony.

A World without Bees

Many bees are struggling to survive. If they die off completely, wild plants and farm crops could lose their important pollinators. The seeds, nuts, fruits, and vegetables that feed animals would disappear. And without reproducing, the plants themselves would fail to spread, leading to fewer leafy shelters that protect small creatures and their young.

Humans would have fewer fruits and vegetables in a bee-free world. We would need to rely more on self- or wind-pollinated crops, such as wheat, corn, and soybeans. Less variety in our diets would make them less nutritious and would likely impact our overall health.

Bees help plants and trees grow. These plants then clean the air. As plants that rely on bees struggle to survive, our planet gets dirtier.

Protecting the Buzz

Today, many groups are working together to try to save this keystone species. Communities are protecting bee habitats and their supply of nectar and pollen. People are planting pollinator-friendly gardens to create safe and nutritious spaces where bees can eat.

As they buzz from flower to flower, bees are working hard. By helping plants grow and spread, these insects are feeding our world. They are helping build homes for many creatures and keeping the planet green. Bees truly are key!

Scientists are trying to understand the stresses and diseases that are harming bees. They are encouraging farmers and landscapers to try using natural alternatives to pesticides and other harmful chemicals.

Save the Bees

It's not too late to save the bees! There are lots of things you can do every day to help protect bees so they can stay busy feeding our world and making it a whole lot greener.

Grow native plants in your yard or garden to support bees. Even a small window box helps.

Bees get thirsty, too! Place stones and pebbles in a shallow bird bath and fill it with water. The stones should stick up out of the water so bees can land on them to take a drink.

Skip pesticides, herbicides, or chemical fertilizers on your lawn or garden. These can harm buzzing bees.

If possible, buy local honey to support the beekeepers in your area.

Educate others! Tell your friends, family, and classmates about all the amazing things bees do, why they are at risk, and why we all should care about their health.

Glossary

colonies groups of animals that live together

domesticated bred and tamed for use by humans

ecosystems communities of animals and plants that depend on one another

enzyme a protein that brings about or speeds up reactions, such as digesting food

extinction when a type of plant or animal dies out completely

mutualists living things that interact in a way that benefits both organisms

native naturally born and living in a particular place

nectar a sweet liquid made by flowers

nutritious having things that an animal or person needs to be healthy

pesticides poisonous chemicals used to kill pests on plants

pollen a colorful dust made by flowers; pollinators help the plants use pollen to make seeds

predators animals that hunt and eat other animals

prey animals that are hunted by other animals for food

reproduce to make more of a living thing

species groups that plants and animals are divided into, according to similar characteristics

venom poison that some animals can send into the bodies of other animals through a bite or sting

Read More

Bergin, Raymond. *Grassland Life Connections (Life on Earth! Biodiversity Explained).* Minneapolis: Bearport Publishing, 2023.

Church, Dana L. *The Beekeepers: How Humans Changed the World of Bumble Bees.* New York: Scholastic Focus, 2021.

Markovics, Joyce. *Bees (Nature's Friends).* Chicago: Norwood House Press, 2023.

Learn More Online

1. Go to **www.factsurfer.com** or scan the QR code below.

2. Enter "**Keystone Bees**" into the search box.

3. Click on the cover of this book to see a list of websites.

Index

About the Author

Olivia was born and raised in Massachusetts but now calls the city of Philadelphia her home. She is a preschool teacher and museum educator. Olivia loves to fill her patio with native plants to feed the bees!